SNOW FALLING ON WATER

Snow Falling on Water

New and Selected Poems by
Richard Taylor

Accents Publishing • Lexington, Kentucky • 2022

Copyright © 2022 by Richard Taylor
All rights reserved

Printed in the United States of America

Accents Publishing
Editor: Katerina Stoykova
Cover Image: Richard Taylor

Library of Congress Control Number: 2022945142
ISBN: 978-1-936628-95-7
First Edition

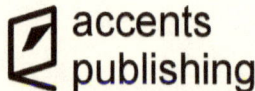

Accents Publishing is an independent press for brilliant voices. For a catalog of current and upcoming titles, please visit us on the Web at

www.accents-publishing.com

CONTENTS

Introduction / ix

Bluegrass (1975)

A Statement of the Case / 3
Masonry / 4
Motorcycle / 5
Premises / 6
The Regionalist / 7
Sunday Afternoon at Mundy's Landing / 8
Frontiers / 9

Girty (1977)

Girty Contemplates the World of Letters / 13
Big Bone Lick / 14
November 1, 1779: First Snow / 15
The Hard Winter / 16
Girty's Vision of the Future / 17
Reconciliation / 18

Earth Bones (1979)

Water Snakes / 21
Bluegills / 23
Lilley's Woods / 24
'52 GMC / 25
Poem for My Father / 26

In the Country of Morning Calm (1998)

The Dialectic of Tedium and Wonder in the Phases of Snow / 29
A Reprieve / 30
Taking Inventory / 32
Fencerow Fandango / 33
Upward Mobility / 34
On Whapping My Index Finger With a Roofing Hammer / 35
The Lava Beds at Pompeii / 36

In Praise of Sycamores / 38
First Monday on Sabbatical / 40

Stone Eye (2001)

Feeding / 43
An Inner Tour of Shaker Village at Pleasant Hill, Kentucky / 45
Refractions / 47
Dreaming the Buffalo Back / 48
Notes Toward a Backyard Bestiary / 49
A Peaks Mill Polemic / 51
A Prescription for Coping With the Next Millennium … / 52
Severn Creek / 53

Rail Splitter: Sonnets on the Life of Abraham Lincoln (2009)

A Man Without a Church / 57
Sojourn in Lexington on Route to Congress / 58
Parallel Lives / 59
Each Great Tree Its Shadow / 60
Assassin / 61

Rare Bird: Sonnets on the Life of John James Audubon (2011)

Derivations / 65
Audubon's Apprenticeship Days in Couëron / 66
Predicting the Passing of the Passenger Pigeon / 67
Squirrel Hunting With Colonel Daniel Boone / 68
The Natural Scheme of Things / 69

Fading Into Bolivia (2011)

Writing Slump / 73
Priming / 74
Grading / 75
Home Repairs / 76
Relationships / 77
Peaks Mill Road / 78

Grand Design / 79
First Anniversary of My Son's Death: April 30, 2004 / 80
New Year / 81

Rain Shadow (2014)

Rain Shadow / 85
Cartography / 86
Plumbing / 87
First Frost / 88
Distinctive / 89
By the Prince Albert Memorial, London / 90
Wild Turkeys / 91
Deliverance / 92
Good Will / 93
In Defense of Letters / 94
Imagining My Own Death / 95
The Origins of Dust / 96

The Feast of Silence (2017)

The Feast of Silence / 99
Mt. Vernon Road / 101
A Trembling in the Leaf / 102
Meeting an Old Friend After 50 Years / 103
Revelation / 104
Instruction / 105
Wildness / 106

New Poems

Mastering the Landscape / 109
Degas's Sketch of a Reclining Figure / 110
Degas / 111
The Task of Restoring Democracy / 112
Attention / 113
Night Driving / 114

Accommodation / 115
Christmas Morning / 116

Acknowledgments / 117
About the Author / 119

INTRODUCTION

Richard Taylor's first book of poems, *Bluegrass*, was published almost 50 years ago, in 1975, by Gray Zeitz at Larkspur Press. The first poem in *Bluegrass* is "A Statement of the Case" and the poem begins with "the words" and details the struggle of language to adequately describe the natural world. Some words "skim to the surface … into voice-giving air." Others are trapped and stalled,

> still others, too many,
> rise to bump horns
> with the sycamore:
>
> outmatched, stuck hopelessly,
> they fret and pitch
> on points of white antlers.

Here, at the beginning of a long and fruitful career as a poet, Taylor is asking very basic questions: how can I participate in the natural world, especially in the world of the wild? what is the function of language in my encounters with that world? what use might my attempts to verbalize my experience be to others, as they enjoin nature in their myriad ways?

Taylor's investigation of the natural world is wide-ranging—animal, vegetable and mineral. He writes about water snakes, turtles, buffalo, pileated woodpeckers, his beloved deer, starlings, snowshoe hares, hawks, moths, spiders, wild turkeys; about sycamores, Virginia bluebells, bamboo, a fallen silver maple, chicory, green tomatoes ripening in paper, yellowing tobacco, thistle, pokeweed; about fog, snow, wind, rain, softened ground, dust, creek, even giving voice to river and rock. Taylor's great teacher, Guy Davenport, said that "art is always the replacement of indifference by attention." Taylor's intense attention and his rendering of that attention into unexpected images and metaphors can startle us and help us see the world differently. Take, for example, this passage about spring from "Severn Creek":

> It's early. Spring purrs its lime
> among the branch tips—not yet
> an exclamation. The trout lily
> has performed its bloom,

> but the Dutchman's breeches
> are still furled like silken flags.
> Fire pinks still smolder
> hours shy of floral combustion,
> the beds of bluebells
> we hiked miles to see
> already basking in the bottoms.

And more lines about spring, from "On Whapping My Index Finger with a Roofing Hammer":

> Spring is still a murmur,
> the yard simmering with patches
> of scrawny green, wands
> in the water maples
> blushing lavender
> against the sober ridge.

These descriptions are alive with image and music, and as we read our sense of spring becomes enlarged, enhanced.

In his autobiography, *The Education of Henry Adams,* Adams refers to himself as a man of the 17th and 18th centuries, who was born in the 19th century and thrust into the 20th. I think of Richard Taylor as a man of the 18th and 19th centuries, born in the 20th century and thrust into the 21st. He reminds me of those erudite and amateur naturalists, geologists, archeologists, astronomers, and historians who populated rural England in the 19th century. His alter egos, all outsiders, are from those centuries: Simon Girty, Sue Mundy, Audubon, Lincoln, Cassius Marcellus Clay. In "A Peaks Mill Polemic," he rails against the modern "tyrannies of plumb and square" and in "To the Tavern-Keeper, Giant Jim Porter, Who Died at Shippingport, Louisville, 1859" he begins, "Jim, it's changed" and concludes,

> The Ohio River Valley is an arena:
> zippers close our pants.
> Crazed with hamburgers,
> we hoot from bleachers to grouse about our death.

He laments the inattentiveness of his students, the distractions of computers and cell phones, Wal-Marts, highways which cross and obliterate the ways of the wild. In "Dreaming the Buffalo Back" his buffalo "reclaim the landscape" as

> they graze resolutely east,
> past patios, through fences
> and staked tomatoes

These dream buffalo triumph, while the actual fate of the buffalo haunts us, reminds us of the worlds we have lost. How do we keep the past alive, use it to make ourselves and our friends more humane, more open to the mystery of our lives?

In Taylor's seventh volume of poems, *Fading Into Bolivia*, a new voice emerges, a much more personal one. He introduces us to this new perspective comically—I should say here that Taylor has a rich comic voice—in the first poem, "Writing Slump." Though the poem is very funny, the subject throughout is loss: the loss of creativity, the loss of his son's stolen car, the loss of his mother's memory. A few pages later this heartbreaking poem, "Love Poem,"

> I am your postage stamp
> licked, applied to paper,
> cancelled, sent far away.
> Feel my serrated edges.

"Relationships" concludes with "everything inside coming out,/ everything outside coming in." We have not heard this voice before. The world has darkened. Taylor's older son has died in a freak accident, his marriage has failed. The world of love and relationships has become *Terra Incognita*. In the concluding poem of this volume, "New Year", his hopes are,

> toward an hour when all that breaks
> is mended, when all the fragments
> that pile in seamless shards
> and little cairns of dust will,

> like unpaired socks and fractured hearts,
> reincorporate with perfect wholeness.

The next volume, *Rain Shadow*, begins with the title poem, a clear description of the two sides of a mountain in Costa Rica. This hearkens back to his earlier nature poems, but ends with these three lines:

> This divide also delineates
> the wide continent of the heart,
> the razory spine of loving/not loving.

"First Frost" surprises us in a similar way:

> The weather has turned.
> There are clumps of frost flowers
> along the road by the lower hill.
> Morning air has the taste of steel in it.
> I would like to be your scarf.

There is a new gravity in these personal poems, which extends to his nature poems and his poems exploring history. Suffering has cultivated his voice, as has the necessity to explore new worlds, begin new relationships, mourn the dead and dying, face mortality. In "The Feast of Silence"—such a wonderful image that is!—his subtle music and fluid images point beyond language, to the mystery of silence. Despite everything, Taylor is able to feel at home in the world and to experience joy. In "Wildness," the final poem of *The Feast of Silence*, the narrator sees two deer whose

> ... muzzles follow my passing car
> until it passes, then dropping their wary gazes
> and bending their necks again, at home
> in the world as it is despite its jarring metal,
> its uncompromising engines, its men
> who pretend they are foliage of summer trees.
> I feel a tingling that begins in the wrists
> and spreads with the joy of them.

Snow Falling on Water is an excellent introduction to Richard Taylor's poems. He writes with deep acumen and great humility about the mysteries of the world, both outer and inner, past and present. A recurrent image in his poems is that of new fallen snow which is then tracked across, leaving us with footprints, an image which becomes a blank page the writer fills with words. Taylor's tracks, his words, are a great blessing and lead us to the possibility of a previously unimagined communion with the world.

—Michael Moran

Bluegrass (1975)

A STATEMENT OF THE CASE

The words sleep under a lid
of water
drowsing near cattail feet.

Rubbed with heat,
they skim to the surface
on fish scales,

break silver
through mats of green algae
into voice-giving air.

But a few, four-winged,
skate up
with the dragonfly.

Still others, too many,
rise to bump horns
with the sycamore:

outmatched, stuck hopelessly,
they fret and pitch
on points of white antlers.

MASONRY

Walls I would build
start where the current
settles its stones,
spots where the bottom
clogs with bedloads
a stream won't tumble.

Limestone laid in
alluvial pockets,
cobbles and blocks
washed clear, silt-free,
hardened wads of every
fossil I ever dreamed.

Lifting them dripping
whole in my hands,
stacking stone on stone,
I trust no mortar
but shape
to give them bond.

If they topple,
if ice from within
buckles them down,
still the channels
are cleared.
Still there is gravity
dared by mass.

MOTORCYCLE

I have a friend named Robert
married and sells insurance
who rode a 650 BSA before his wife
declared it a hazard.
Now, twice a month, regular
as premiums, he upends
a bottle of Jack Daniel's
dreams of donning his jeans
and old boots and tooling that bike
to Pauline's whorehouse
in Bowling Green, Kentucky.
When he rides, he changes
his name to Jesse.

PREMISES

What we're looking for
is a place
with none of the conveniences.
Where the rocks
have not trimmed their nails.

Our needs are few—
some bedrock, some water,
a view of the moon:
tadpoles swim in the print
of one hoof.

What we don't find
we'll scavenge and build.
We'll bring our own tools
and plant by the signs.

All we are asking is
a goldfinch in the chicory.

THE REGIONALIST

His range he pared
to an absolute core
of manageable stars.
His accent turned juniper.
The moon left his nails.

Each spring he barged down
the thaw on flowering stones
& black-bottomed
with a snowshoe hare.

Body and soul, he shuffled
that widow, flung muskrats
up from their beds.

When he came to rest,
he held so still
moss nosed out
on his northern slope.

SUNDAY AFTERNOON AT MUNDY'S LANDING

Breeze off the river stirs the leaves
of a sycamore overhead.
A few shed saffron on the green water.
They look like hands.
Where the ferry crossed toward Troy
is a heap of mussel shells
cluttering the bank like broken spoons.
The river laps cold at my feet.
Not a bird, not a sound,
no gauge to cipher moment from moment
until across the river
an outboard fails, sputters, then catches.
Tomorrow, at the library, they will be angry
that the books are overdue.

FRONTIERS

I want to pass easy,
with as little stir
as the blue lobe of locust shade,
the cool where cows gather,
that dusk deepens into.

Girty (1977)

GIRTY CONTEMPLATES THE WORLD OF LETTERS

I stare at the page,
the words like tiny boots
their heels in snow,
tracks I can't make or follow.
Words fur my head.
They weave thick weaves
and pelt my bones.
They shrivel when I stretch.
My comfort to know
you will know me not by tracks
but only by some skins
I've shed.

BIG BONE LICK

I feel the bones of great beasts
sucking through the ooze,
the furry souls of mammoths
terraced in the muck,
tongues of jealous fossils
itching for my salt.

Among the bone herds
poking from the marsh
are 10-pound tapir skulls,
tusks of arctic elephants
curved gracefully as swans.

I stretch my tent
on borrowed ribs,
I bunk on ivory spines.
My sleep is strung with broken peals,
trapped mammals sticky
in my dreams,
extinction and the Age of Ice
nudging at my meat.

NOVEMBER 1, 1779: FIRST SNOW

A sense of beginnings.
The light more intense.
Sound furred in deep shawls.
The slopes purified of all detail.
The snow made literate with my feet.

THE HARD WINTER

The Hard Winter of 1779
snow rose to our waists
before it froze
Rivers lockt hands
Creeks went crystal stiff
with diamond fish

Wind blew so chill
brutes sang in the woods
The maples split & crackt
like pistols
Frost bit green cane
& rain fell frigid needles

It turned so cold
tirkies tumbled off their roosts
& broke like china
Cows hugged chimneys
till the mucus
in their nostrils froze

I lost one toe

GIRTY'S VISION OF THE FUTURE

I see the corn in puckered rows
the stumps of squandered trees
the landscape tamed with fences
ruts cut by metal wheels.

I see the skulls of buffalo,
bone commas stacked in piles,
plucked turkey wings & Indian hair,
words twisting black as rivers.

The land made fit for Christians,
stiff trophies on each wall,
the hobby of extinction
made universal law.

RECONCILIATION

The sleep I sleep
is gorged with war,
my dreams are charred
as droves of bony widows
scrape their razors on my door,
lay orphans at my feet.

Waking now to milky light,
the cabin blanched with mutton snow,
my world made chaste again,
through window glaze my breath melts
I squint to see my speckled hen,
that beauty
balanced on one sacrificial leg,
the other lifted snug in feathers
as she hops off one and then the other
in deference to the cold.

The truce she makes
I make my own.
I shift my stance
I change my gait,
I dress to suit the weather.

The perfect friction with the world
is snow that falls on water.

Earth Bones (1979)

WATER SNAKES

Winter for them is pause,
a space between suns,
another skin to shed.

Each spring three or four
turn up on the ledges
under the bridge,

revived commas wriggling
to catch
the earliest sun.

As the rocks grow warmer,
some slide off to clumps
of wild parsley,

their steel backs freckling
with delicate shade,
riddled with light.

Scale cipher, hieroglyph,
something keeps
drawing me back.

Daily I edge to the rail,
craning over to stare
on insolent fat of the biggest,

coiled muscles that tremor
on minnows and frogs,
knobs of dwindling flesh.

Or fixed to one smaller,
dangling efficiently in water,
aloof in all currents:

its white head emerging,
the unblinking eyes—
this creek its necklace.

BLUEGILLS

Barely visible,
they blend so well,

their glossed scales
merge with light.

Bass know them only
by their telltale shadows,

blunt-tipped cigars
that nose along the bottom,

light snacks slipped from cover
to flit past bedrock,

cross sulfurous leaf
and silt mound, trembling.

LILLEY'S WOODS

Oaks and hemlocks,
highland maples,
tight-skinned beeches,
virgins so sheltered
what sun there is leaks through,
green seepage
ladled down to dogwoods,
spoon-fed to ferns.

Staggered in tiers,
the leaves span out
to grab
each rill of light,
to palm
each lagging limb
browned and cancelled
by emphatic shade.

Clobbered by lightning
or slow-drilled to humus
they climax
and topple,
their downfalls
clearing new swaths,
vacancies
which fill
with eager seed.

'52 GMC

Running my pickup is like Emperor Maximilian
winning and holding the Mexican Empire:
no matter how secure the capital,
rebellion always flares in one of the provinces.

POEM FOR MY FATHER

Days after his death
we found the faith he left us
in the shed:

six late tomatoes
shining on the sill,
stems carefully plucked,
green skins to the sun,

the last of his garden
surviving frost
to ripen in our blood.

In the Country of Morning Calm (1998)

THE DIALECTIC OF TEDIUM AND WONDER IN THE PHASES OF SNOW

At first, who isn't dazzled?
The backyard's drab particulars
revert to elementary dunes,
billows and swags
that lap against the hillside—
a glittering manifesto.
Humped with snow, the dwarf magnolia
dissolves miraculously into the ridgeline.
The field beyond is *tabula rasa*,
a span of untracked innocence.

But purity wears. We find
monotony in the frugal slopes,
a white hyperbole
that deprives as it illuminates.
Whether by inches or the foot,
snow becomes nothing so much
as bland assertion.

What we crave before the day is out
are definition, contrast, thaw—
a renaissance of shadow,
another dawn with landmarks,
earthly smudges, some dark repatriation.

A REPRIEVE

Just at dusk
as we drive back from town,
my two sons in the rear seat
squabbling over videos,
two deer—one doe and a leery buck—
step, almost prance,
hooves clicking onto the asphalt,
their legs, thin as spindles,
chiseled precisely
against the slopes of pristine snow.

My headlights hold the bronze
of their eyes, coals that glow
across evolutionary spans
to the embers of the first fire,
a first skirmish with the unknowable.
The engine is running.
My beams skewer through the dark
to pierce an animal calm
that ill-adapts them to this century.

This sad road severs theirs.
Three new houses gone up on the ridge
whittle their passage down
to a corridor of dark
amid a galaxy of porchlights,
a bluish sheen in the windows
where first the fields held sway.

I brake as the doe
skitters off the roadway
and clears the wire fence
into the bachelor farmer's chaste acres.

Vacillating, the buck stands
enchanted in the glare,
unsure whether to brave the beams
and follow or shy back
toward the undivided dark.

And then, from behind,
Willis shouts, awed
by some force Nintendo
can't prepare us for,
"Did you see that?
He jumped the fence!
He jumped the fence!"

Turning, I just glimpse the spectacle,
some vague articulation of grace
as the buck for an instant glides,
then lights, bounds off
in the harboring dark,
the scruffy flash of his upright tail
a sign of hazard and triumph—
some force, some mystery
that eludes the highest fence,
the brightest hill,
and grants us all reprieve.

TAKING INVENTORY

A week before Christmas
I canvass the woods
along the lower hill,
taking stock of gains and losses—
what wind or malady laid low.

This season it's a buckeye,
broad and stiff as a skillet,
its brittle crown snapped
like a pretzel
into the crotch of a sickly elm
whose shagged limbs
yaw and tremble under the yoke.

I prune off what I can,
this surgery
not just to exalt the living
or lighten the strain
but to bring the dead
decently down—to complete
what gravity and ripeness began.

As the butt end is swung,
drops clear, this sad elm
shivers, visibly shrugs,
then recomposes.
Limber as wands,
its branch tips spray back,
reassemble, triggered by some
inner spring, some yen for light,
that reassembles us.

FENCEROW FANDANGO

What I'm drawn to
is not the stuff of cultivated fields,
the homogeneous plenty, say,
of sorghum or sweet corn—
petty kingdoms of pure utility.

Lured by richer yields,
I turn to fencerow pockets—
lush ghettos—the gypsy fringe
of smilax, thistle, poke,
a rendezvous where nomads
mingle, splurge,
home of the wandering spore.

Here are no tampering hands
no predictable outcomes,
but instead a no man's land
of ardent fronds and laissez-faire.
Left to itself, this green caucus
plays no favorites, bestows no crowns.
Sometimes the cherry seedling pries entry
through the honeysuckle vines.
Sometimes it doesn't.

UPWARD MOBILITY
for A.R. Ammons

Given your druthers,
I said to the rock,
what is it you would most
like to have that is man's?
Is it a tower of bone
from which to lord it over the others?
Is it reason, virtue, a face
that is the mirror of God's,
an opposable thumb?

Oh no, said the rock.
Those heights where the air
is anemic are nothing to me,
and dialectic puts me to sleep—
give me wind any day over babble.
Having little use for the upright,
I prefer proneness, my niche
on the slopes. Sedentary ways.
Admitting that much is beyond
my grasp, still I know God's face
at the head of the hollow
is a craggy wonder.
When it rains, when it washes,
I take note of the flow,
but mostly I keep to my stratum,
resting frugal and flat.
All right, mundane. But
indispensably mundane.

ON WHAPPING MY INDEX FINGER WITH A ROOFING HAMMER

This time it happens on the garage
nailing shingles, driving
steel on steel through asphalt, felt,
and poplar sheathing tacked down
before McKinley was shot.

Spring is still a murmur,
the yard simmering with patches
of scrawny green, wands
in the water maples
blushing lavender
against the sober ridge.

From his pickup window
Jim Haney waves, yells up
to ask if I'm doing any good—
just enough distraction
to skew the dropping hammer,
his wife and teenage daughter
wincing in the cab
when I shout the most basic verb
that pain can summon.

Yowling, offending the righteous—
imprecision has other costs.
Add the cuticle's shattered moon,
the blue-back scarab
already trapped beneath the nail.
This throbbing cannot match
even one forsythia
whose swollen buds muscled just now
their yellow liberation into bloom.

THE LAVA BEDS AT POMPEII

Using a steel rod, Giuseppe Fiorelli
first tapped the crust in 1863,
finding hollows where humans
had dried up and all but vanished.
In these pockets he poked holes,
filling the curious voids with plaster.

When it set, he pried out
a plaster man, suffocating,
clawing at his underclothes,
then another clutching some coins.
Next, a woman hugging a child,
two gladiators doomed in their cells,
still manacled to the wall,
even a dog straining at its leash.

What they hold in common
is August 24, 79 A.D., a day
when morning went night
and rained pumice, rivers
of volcanic ash flowing down
the Via dell'Abbondanza
to smother it under twenty feet
of sulfuric silt.

Street by street, yard by yard,
Fiorelli reclaimed what he could:
black loaves from the baker's oven,
a cup unfinished on the potter's wheel,
a table set for noon.
Now, after two millennia,
the victims plead through museum glass,
still writhe against extinction,

affirming all that is human
in the tension of an upraised hand,
a gaping mouth—
agonies more eloquent than speech.

IN PRAISE OF SYCAMORES
For David Orr (1942-1989)

Mention that tree around here
and you summon up Paul Sawyier,
our local impressionist
whose creekscapes blaze with sycamores,
gaudy lemons and ochers
that burn in some eternal summer,
their broad leaves shimmering
above the placid nooks
of some angler's dream.

Cross-grained, unsplittable,
their wood makes butchers' blocks
and not much else
beyond nourishment for the eye—
a blue heaven for the artist.
Lugging only his paint kit, bedroll,
and a tin of nightcrawlers,
Sawyier vanished for days up Elkhorn Creek
to commit his gentle arsons,
constellations of briars starring
the worsteds above his scruffy boots.

Each sycamore is the product of place.
Elbowed by neighbors along the creek,
its crown is vase-shaped, almost modest,
its stem as columnar as swans.
But on open ground it spreads
in pearly tiers like antlers,
its twists and goose-necked spirals
elegant as candelabra,
the trophy of some buried stag.

Winter's tree,
its bark is winter's flag,
an utterance of ice.

Unlike the cedar,
its architecture does not tame itself
to models, will not repeat.
Answering only to persuasions
of rainfall and light,
of soil and creekside rivals,
it persists
as a miscellany of upthrust limbs
whose scoured bark,
gleaming brilliantly white
against the somber hills,
has tracings as precise and eloquent
as veins on the anatomist's chart,
an embroidery that stitch for stitch
knits up the creek
with filigree and frill
to lend the valleys hereabout
some luster, some civility.

FIRST MONDAY ON SABBATICAL

For nearly an hour this morning,
I listen to the steady rain
as it beads along the eaves
and patters to the walk
in detonations small, irregular,
that language has no word for.

These lavish seepings that soak
the tree hydrangea to its roots,
that ping the bucket blue,
free us from the human drive
to measure things, to fit
the rhythms of this world to rhyme.

These plashes, this seething vibrato,
shape the morning
only in their constancy:
wordless, tactile, wetly random.

Stone Eye (2001)

FEEDING

As snowflakes this morning feather
across the backyard and stick
like foundered moths, the first junco
zips onto the grain-filled feeder,

swivels its wary head, and snaps up
a sunflower seed. It's followed
by a white-jowled chickadee
flitting in from the fencerow,

then finches and towhees that perch,
partake, and go about their business,
each levered bill clinching
its kernel of modest heat.

This sequence of civility extends
till in swoops a pushy cardinal,
a red bruiser that scatters
the small-wings. In their chittering,

in the nervous chafings
of their cumulative wings
we read petitions for relief,
comeuppance, a *deus ex machina*

that arrives in the form
of a pileated woodpecker
whose bulk and thrashing wings
displace the displacer,

all of us pausing for moments—
among the slanting flecks,
the chill air enveloping
our accelerated hearts—

with only transparencies of glass
between us, forks suspended
above the cooling pasta
and our own fragile plates.

AN INNER TOUR OF SHAKER VILLAGE
AT PLEASANT HILL, KENTUCKY

In the Center Family dwelling
where the brethren and sisters
ascend to dream on separate stairs,
I feel an invisible razory line
that splits the sexes.
It hovers among the dust motes
that drift toward immaculate floors.
It populates the air, weighs
down the segregated tables
off which the Shakers consumed
their bounty in communal silence—
only a snicking of tableware
unsettling their pious concentration.

Even from the peepholes
where the elders scrutinized
the sabbath dancers,
who stamped and wriggled
with the zeal of martyrs
as they shook off Satan,
there must have been carnal lapses—
infractions of the lingering eye,
lust among the cabbages,
or glimmerings over aqua jars
filled with the jellied plum
and fallen peach, or furtive touchings
as flax seeds were packeted
to green the Lower South.

Though records show Mahalia Polly,
frustrated in marriage five times,
finally eloped with a village miller,
the evidence admits few 'private unions.'

Instead, the Believers must have thrived
on remembered warmth, the heat
preserved in stone walls after sundown.

Into each room sunlight shines—
the same splendor that kissed
the gritty road down which lay
what they described ingenuously
as 'the world.' Inside each room
there is an anteroom, a closet
with an inner window
lit so long as there are beams
of outside radiance, but dimmer,
fainter, still sufficient—what
students of design now refer to,
with praise, as 'borrowed light.'

REFRACTIONS

Winter sunlight shimmies
through the bay window
this morning, its restless photons
jostled by streamers of heat
that rise above the radiator.

These extravagant phantoms
forage along the walls.
They pleat the air
with vibrancies, devising worlds
cryptic and unmappable,
like water riffling over rock.

Lean swimmers, refugees,
their shimmerings romance
the glass-topped table.
They carom off the lampshade,
sprawl across the rug. For an instant,
they hover over the armchair
like stippled trout, then skim
along the dark fonts of the page.

In the anatomy of sunlight,
these shaky halos are the heart,
the shadow's necessary edge.

DREAMING THE BUFFALO BACK

In droves their swollen humps
rise from the shallows, hooves
nicking the asphalt with tiny moons.

Tracking the scent of salt,
they graze resolutely east,
past patios, through fences
and staked tomatoes
toward Stamping Ground,
the bowl-shaped wallow
where they will hunker and swill.

Muzzle to tail, they migrate.
To Sulphur Lick and Great Crossing,
to all the places that carry
their lost names. Shaggy pilgrims,
bearded, robed in snow,
they bunch at night
to blanket their quaking calves.

Under a spatterwork of stars
they herd in the lush pasturage
of dream. Without predators,
they reclaim the landscape
encompassed between the parentheses
of their upturned horns.
Loosed from memory,
they cannot even dream
the space where we might be.

NOTES TOWARD A BACKYARD BESTIARY

Described as stay-at-homes
that seldom range beyond a radius
of two hundred yards,
box turtles keep profiles
so low the hatchmarks
enameled on their horny shells
fuse with litter on the forest floor.

Those not pulped on highways
lead torpid lives that stretch
beyond the oldest humans.
Solitary, domed, they burrow
in the mulch—sensibly sedentary,
unavoidably local.

Now science tells us
that a segment of the males—
red-eyed, randy—
seasonally turn rogue,
striking out always due southwest,
tilting shells to copulate
with every female they meet.

To explain this rift in turtledom,
such hardshell wanderlust, experts
hypothesize some evolutionary pulse,
some memory in the blood
that goads the mavericks on.
These promiscuous rambles that
so upend the status quo
disseminate, sow beneficial seeds.

Such goings-on are hardly new,
showing up in vertebrate histories
as modes long endorsed

by Hernán Cortés, by Captain Cook.
And sublimated in one footworn
fellow traveler, the pomological wizard
John 'Appleseed' Chapman, gent.

A PEAKS MILL POLEMIC

The city presumes upon the country.
Its tyrannies of plumb and square
suppress the eye. The blue florescence
above Walmart swarms with insects
that pelt against the stanchions,
their wings snapping in the imperial glare.

Even at midnight, road hum
undermines the crickets,
assaults the last citadels of calm.
The fields lay bare against a siege
that presses from the inside out.
Oil is its instrument.

*A PRESCRIPTION FOR COPING
WITH THE NEXT MILLENNIUM
IN ONE SENTENCE OR LESS*

With no known remedy
for the millennial jitters
in all its predications
of planetary doom—
cyber glitches, jinxed aircraft,
unchartable tides of giddy
rapture, and global warming
that simmers to a cosmic boil—

I improvise as I go, having
tailored no special strategy
to survive digital disruption,
seismic rumblings, or sudden
shifts of psychic ballast

other than to tighten the laces
on my sneakers and take careful
sightings from one landmark
to the next—a pond, a melon patch,
or just another feathery ridge—
inching toward
the Great Millennial Divide
at a pace one savvy neighbor,
a genius at decrypting
contradictory signs, describes
as a "passionate mosey."

SEVERN CREEK

for Gray Zeitz, Larkspur Press

For the third spring we trek
the disused county road,
deer prints pressing ground
made soft by yesterday's showers.
In gray tiers, hardwoods rise up
toward the cedared bluffs.
The luscious glut of creek water
riffles through us intimate as breath.

It's early. Spring purrs its lime
among the branch tips—not yet
an exclamation. The trout lily
has performed its bloom,
but the Dutchman's breeches
are still furled like silken flags.
Fire pinks still smolder
hours shy of floral combustion,
the beds of bluebells
we hiked miles to see
already basking in the bottoms.

As we pass a bank of larkspurs,
each spiked floret asserting
its purple integrity, its tensile grace,
Gray, inspired, declares this occasion
the annual meeting of his board.

With a simple show of hands
the membership, each spring, each
spacious leaf, reaffirms its policy
to vegetate the hills,

following by-laws to the letter
with each corporate tendril,
each dash of color, as we all assent
to raise, to resurrect, the dead.

Rail Splitter: Sonnets on the Life of Abraham Lincoln
(2009)

A MAN WITHOUT A CHURCH

Belonging to no church except his conscience,
Lincoln, a suspected deist, kept his own counsel
with God. Stump rivals said no Christians ought
to go for him, especially Peter Cartwright,
a circuit-riding Methodist who wanted the seat
himself and whispered infidelity. Responding,
Lincoln drafted a handbill, claiming he followed
a "doctrine of necessity," our minds impelled
to action or checked by some power a mind could
not control, some brand of fatalism. When he nervily
took a back pew in Cartwright's church after a day
of stumping, candidate Cartwright challenged him
to say where he was going, if not to heaven, if not
to hell. "To Congress," Lincoln said. And did.

SOJOURN IN LEXINGTON ON ROUTE TO CONGRESS

For three weeks the congressman-elect, his wife, his boys, were hosted by his in-laws, strangers nearly, in their privileged habitat. "Little Sister" Emilie, on first meeting, saw the giant of Jack's story of the beanstalk. Through Todds he met his idol Henry Clay and heard him blast the war with Mexico as empire-building. In their library he learned by heart Mr. Bryant's "Thanatopsis," whose fatalistic musings on earth as the "great tomb of man" invigorated him with melancholy. Here he witnessed slavery at its mildest but saw just down the street Lewis Robards' slave pens where humans were commodities as much as cabbages. More, a bruised cabbage wouldn't sell.

PARALLEL LIVES

Born same year, same day, Darwin as pigeon
fancier, student of barnacles, orchids, earthworms,
showed how genius journeys on separate paths.
Texts tells us Lincoln put one rebellion down, that
Darwin sparked another, unseating God, unseating
man as a species special, central, fixed, & favored.
In the business, finally, of loosening chains from
bodies, Lincoln had little time to ponder Darwin's
freeing minds, an enterprise that split the union
of man and God as science made blind nature king,
a view that would have titillated Lincoln. How
the gentleman naturalist must have marveled
at the news of Lincoln's end—America taking
exception to the law that the best, the fittest, last.

EACH GREAT TREE ITS SHADOW

Death courted Lincoln all his days, starting
with his father's mare that kicked him cold
and speechless, hoof to forehead, as he coaxed
her with a whip to turn some grist at Gordon's
Mill. Or when a neighbor raised him sodden
from a swollen creek within a gasp of drowning.
High office brought so many threats he stashed
them in a special file, *Assassination*, knowing
those who threatened seldom acted, those that
acted seldom threatened, convinced he could not
dodge the fatal bullet, bomb, or knife, flesh being
flesh, the world being a place where things
happened by necessity, by design, sure as
rainfall running off his roof in beaded curtains.

ASSASSIN

How long Booth had it in for Lincoln isn't clear,
but there were signs and sightings long before
the final act. For months obsession held him,
first to kidnap as a bargaining chip to end the war,
then to simply do him in. Off stage & on, the man
was charismatic, a conspirator's conspirator,
a compass whose needle, though it swung erratic,
always targeted north. "He makes me thrill,"
said son Tad, who'd heard and seen him strut—
to whom the actor presented a rose in tribute.
At the inaugural, a close-up of the crowd reveals
a hatted madman within spitting distance of the
rostrum. Booth's father's middle name was
Brutus, the Roman who killed that other Caesar.

Rare Bird: Sonnets on the Life of John James Audubon
(2011)

DERIVATIONS

Both Audubons, *pere et fils*, worked to keep
the painter's origins as vague as Homer's,
his sea captain father to mask his infidelity
& the sting of bastardy, his son for reasons
as much romantic as politic, never deflating
the rumor that he was the Lost Dauphin,
heir to France, even fudging on his birthplace—
not Sainte-Dominique to a creole chambermaid
but continental Louisiana, a territory soon
to be a state & so ease the way to citizenship,
a means to dodge the draft during Napoleon's
drive for empire. He would be the first to claim
that genius has no homeland, no pedigree,
no place of birth, no rank, no father, mother.

AUDUBON'S APPRENTICESHIP DAYS IN COUËRON

Discovering what would be his life's work
In a book of illustrations Papa gave him,
Jay Jay woke one morning with an urge
to copy nature, to replicate what country
rambles couldn't save—a nest, a speckled
egg, the luster on a lapwing. He learned
that pigment dabbed with water endowed
the curlew's eye with life and held it fresh,
untainted. "A family of cripples" he likened
his early efforts to, a roll call of the maimed
he burned each birthday, holding only
a lust, a joy, to keep what wouldn't keep,
a deep-felt animus through art to resurrect
the dead—each species, every sketch, a Lazarus.

PREDICTING THE PASSING OF THE PASSENGER PIGEON

For this graceful species Jay Jay figured more
as chiding witness than agent of extinction.
By his *Belle Riviere* at Henderson he reckoned
over a billion in a single flock, passing quick
as thought inside coils of a gigantic serpent
whose "aerial evolutions" blotted out the sun,
their living wind "a feathered tempest," their
wing buzz nearly lulling him to sleep. Farmers
shot these "Blue Meteors" from their roosts
to fatten hogs, others clubbing with poles
to pluck tailpins for the trade ladies' hats.
With such "dreadful havock," Jay Jay foresaw
an end to earth's fastest living things, their
wing flaps, like a gale through rigging, stilled.

SQUIRREL HUNTING WITH COLONEL DANIEL BOONE

That Jay Jay saw D. Boone anywhere but
in his imagination's meadow is doubtful, yet
he claimed to witness in a stand of nut trees
by waters of the Kentucky the master "bark"
a squirrel, killing his dinner by concussion
rather than disturb the flesh, misdescribing
the marksman as a barrel-chested Atlas,
when the man behind the legend was sinewy,
slight, and in Missouri, self-exiled from a state
in which he owned not one discovered acre.
Witnessed, unwitnessed, Jay Jay must have
marveled at the frontier wonder's skill
& envied—his own remedy for smaller birds
being smaller shot and illusion, an artist's
tool to mask the carnage of charged metal.

THE NATURAL SCHEME OF THINGS

Jay Jay saw nature as a kind of bank
In which each deposit and withdrawal
upheld a touchy balance. Take his purple
grackles that pillage unripe corn. Their
subtle hues, a silky iridescence that paint
can never replicate, are banditry's pageant.
Through his cracked bill the male raises
exultant squawks, his nest-mate perched
on huskings of a ravaged ear, her beak
pinching one filched kernel for her brood.
Mindful of the bird's "nefarious propensities,"
Jay Jay marvels at the play of light, a gloss
unfolding from coppery bronze to azure,
from sapphire to emerald green in synergies
that stun. In this equation, beauty forgives
marauding as an act of necessary plunder,
simple commerce, as if to say, "Borrow, lend."

Fading Into Bolivia (2011)

WRITING SLUMP

As I drive to work, the sky is void
as though the clouds have seceded
to compose their own republic of rain.

The red fox that scurried across
the road last week, the one I'd been saving
for a poem, insists she's only a red fox.

Even the puddles from yesterday's shower
metallic and flat as spatulas, shrug off
light and hold the shadows hostage.

I imagine my son's stolen Honda
being dismantled in some chop shop,
an automotive diaspora, its disc player

surgically transplanted, radials married
to a pickup, say in Alabama, hub caps
migrating to some Valhalla of chrome.

Something will come, I tell myself.
Still, the mimosa holds its tongue,
its punker pink blossoms speechless.

In an act of unwitting collaboration
that describes her state and mine,
my mother calls to say, "Some days
I feel I'm fading into Bolivia."

PRIMING

After the last gasping commentary
on the Super Bowl, after awarding
a final wedge of pizza to the dogs,
kids bedded, house secure,
pencil ground to a razory stave,

I sink into the worn armchair
by the front window
where moonlight glimmers
among the maples, each limb
traced indelibly in snow.

As stillness settles the restless neurons—
the small change of shopping lists,
the exigent trifles of morning and work—
I measure the snowy tundra
that rises toward the ridgeline,
the untracked expanse of paper
resting on my lap.

Waiting for what comes to come,
what goes to go,
I brace to front the weather—
bundled, blank, disburdened—
at last, reduced to words.

GRADING

Reading term papers in my armchair
by the window this December morning.

I trudge an endless trail of print,
switch-backing down and across

page after page after page,
faltering in brambles of prose

that pile in mental drifts and vanish
from the path, no destination in sight.

Outside, the dogs skitter over new-fallen
snow, yipping and reveling in its simple,

perfect whiteness, their pawprints
swerving, halting, going this way, that.

HOME REPAIRS

Measuring for a new countertop
of black granite,

studying paint charts and testing
six subtle shades of avocado
on the kitchen wall,

replacing naked florescent tubes
with a natty overhead
in the style of art nouveau,

shoring up the side porch
to bring it into plumb, erasing
swags along the roofline—

my wife is making
so many improvements
I don't sleep well at night.

RELATIONSHIPS

Like kayaks, they float best
when kept nose to the current,
buoyant and free of drift.

When they dip and take on water,
they wobble and won't respond,
which paddling hard won't alter.

Unable to maneuver past rocks,
under raking limbs, through swells,
unable to right or seek new channels,

impossible to bail in choppy water
when listing, they tump or founder,
everything inside coming out,
everything outside coming in.

PEAKS MILL ROAD

In the near dark where the doe lies,
half on, half off the road,
my headlights come on to the survivors:
two bucks, a spotted fawn,
and two or three vague others.

Ears tensed, sleek heads swiveling
in the glare, hooves as lustrous,
edged, and deadly as a shot glass,
they find no refuge in shadow,
the brightness welding them together.

They do not break. They do not scatter.

From the doe's ripped pelage,
from the head wedged
into a clump of blue chicory,
from the unfamiliar fixity
of her yellow eye, they raise
their own unblinking gaze.

New to this new country,
they lift their muzzles to the night.
They sniff at death's shore.

GRAND DESIGN

The oldest narratives have no name.
They come down to us in patterns
as natural, as variable, as rain,

needing little to thread them into sense.
Picture a farmer in the wide bottom near
Peaks Mill on a Sunday mowing hay,

his engine droning along a stand
of waist-high alfalfa, sickling it down
in shrinking grids, a stricken doe

nearby, her tail aloft in white alarm,
a clutch of five or six turkey vultures
huddled and bent among the cuttings,

neither I nor my friend acknowledging
as we pass a formula so ancient, pat,
we do not need to see or verify to say
the word we need not say: fawn.

FIRST ANNIVERSARY OF MY SON'S DEATH: APRIL 30, 2004

Stepping into the room where books
are shelved, I feel a ruffling of ether
that signifies another chimney swift
has found its way inside without an exit.
Instead of the usual flurry, the frantic
bumping against the window's brittle sky,
this one lights on the molding
above Truman Capote and Willa Cather.

Its beak crooks open to accommodate
either liberty or death. There is no need
to reposition the ladder that leans,
small wonder, in perfect alignment.

Towel in hand, I rise up rungs and cup
the unresisting pod of feathers, wings
folded into itself, eyes unblinking,
its heartbeat steady and persistent as grief.

Outside, exposed in the valley of my hands,
for an instant it pauses to assess the air
then sails off through tiered limbs
toward a greenness beyond my seeing.

Each flap of its scalloped wings, each
scissoring stroke as it blends into the tree line,
drives home the single unspoken text:
"Let it go. Let it go. Let it go."

NEW YEAR

On a shelf in the pantry
I save all the dinnerware
I've broken during the year:
a handleless ceramic mug,
a plain but favored butter dish,
a tulip-shaped wine glass
severed from its stem, flowers
hand-painted around its bowl.

Though I know I'll never restore
them, never probably try,
and that no glue will form

a bond to withstand the tensions
of dishwater or even ceremonial use,
still I stack them, china casualties,

toward an hour when all that breaks
is mended, when all the fragments
that pile in seamless shards
and little cairns of dust will,
like unpaired socks and fractured hearts,
reincorporate with perfect wholeness.

Rain Shadow (2014)

RAIN SHADOW
Guanacaste, Costa Rica

From the black volcanic
tip of the isthmus's highest mountains
we can survey, east and west,
two bodies of water
separated only by a narrow bench
of green and two ribbons of white surf
where the waters lap but never join.

One side of the mountain
is drenched and verdant, a riot of green—
its plush canopy unbroken for miles—
the other parched by what meteorologists
call *rain shadow*, its barren slope
arid with elfin thickets of stunted growth
that thirst in sullen expectation.

This divide also delineates
the wide continent of the heart,
the razory spine of loving/not loving.

CARTOGRAPHY

When maps were pilots' guides to silk or glory,
cartographers added at least one *trap line*,
one imaginary place, somewhere falsely named
to thwart those who pirated them into print.
You are mine. Following your contours in all
your loops and nooses, your varying elevations,
I trip across your trap line. Close to home,
my compass shivers, its needle pointing
this way, that, toward some imagined landfall.
Zigging, zagging, switching tack, I scrape bottom,
pass rocks that boulder into sea beasts. Your West
is *Terra Incognita*, true destinations marked only
on your master map. A haze ahead, behind,
I bump along your coast, a citizen of salt.

PLUMBING

> I consider love the most beautiful thing
> on earth ... and find nourishment in illusion.
> I don't think illusions are totally vain but
> rather that they are ... substantial and innate
> in all of us—and they form the whole of our life.
>
> —Giacomo Leopardi, Pensieri

You are the mispaired handles on twin pipes
feeding the tap of my disused downstairs tub—
a claw-footed relic without a head for showers.
What reads H is actually cold and never warms.
C, in fact, is scalding hot. Knowing that I twist
neither often enough to get things right by custom
or that I'm too hopelessly conditioned by what I read
to swap them out, the result is recurrent surprise,
an unretired mystery, a state of use that keeps—
like swings of mood or unaccountable whim—
what comes out predictably unpredictable.
What is love, or life, if not a test of illusion
and faith, a readiness to accept what may not be,
what isn't said, the burnt hand reaching out again?

FIRST FROST

The weather has turned.
There are clumps of frost flowers
along the road by the lower hill.
Morning air has the taste of steel in it.
I would like to be your scarf.

DISTINCTIVE

From a beekeeper
I learn that honey from each hive
has its own taste,
its own distinctive flavor
based on diet or weather,
a late frost snuffing
white flowers of the black locust,
a lean harvest of local rain,
or maybe a stricken queen—
differences on the tongue
as near as the next field,
depending on what each forager
is drawn to plunder,
which turns in part
on what blossoms when, where, if.

This explains much,
including how each of us
becomes each.

BY THE PRINCE ALBERT MEMORIAL, LONDON

A woman wearing a sari, a daub
of holiness on her forehead,
stands on a traffic island
in the mechanical din of rush hour.

I am standing marooned
on my own island, between us
a narrow chasm of slicing metal.

As the signals change, our eyes meet.
The green effigy in the signal box
starts blinking, and the numbers
flash their countdown before us.

As she steps forward, I see what
she doesn't—one last traffic bandit
trying to brass his way through.

Before her sandaled foot can step
into disaster,
I flash my own warning—
maybe raising a hand
but probably not—
enough for her to read
the glare of admonition in my eye.

Her foot retracts to the safety
of the curb. The car, opaque behind
its steely shimmering, zooms past.

Again, our eyes meet,
affirming something prelingual that crowns
the history of our species on the planet.

WILD TURKEYS

Rushed to reach the dentist's
and scratch one more item
off my list of things to do,
I hurry down the porch steps,
stopping, car door half open,
as I glance beyond the porch steps,
to see not one or two, but seven turkeys
foraging on the hillside,
lean, each cupped in its feathery sheen
like ancient scales or bark,
each going its own unruffled way,
wattled bills picking who knows
what—seeds or insects—
except one preening in the sunlight,
wings flexed open in air languor,
clear ground between it
and anything like harm.
They gabble. They dip
with each mincing step
as though warming to flightlessness.
Slowly, in some long association
dyed deep in the wing,
in a tongue for which
there are no words,
they answer to light,
working their way upward
toward the tree line at the crest,
past the furry shadow of a lone cedar.
Whichever way they turn is home.

DELIVERANCE

> Be kind to everyone you meet,
> for we are all fighting a great battle.
>
> —Philo of Alexandria

Finding two moths—cousins of those
that gnawed the shoulder off the jacket
I wear to weddings and funerals—
trapped on my screened-in porch this morning,
wings batting against the tiny grids,
agitated like prayer flags before a storm—
I cup one, then the other, in the haven
of my hands, ushering each past
the door jamb into unencumbered air—
in releasing them, releasing all of us.

GOOD WILL

Each mid-afternoon this winter
through my half-opened office blinds
I see a stooped man
who comes to the lot next door,
strewing chunks of bread from a Kroger bag.

Carefully, he tears the crusts into crumbs
and spreads them under limbs of an evergreen.
They catch the eye,
forming white archipelagos
among the dry needles
in a place where snow never falls.

Winter's priest, he wears an oversized parka
that is electric blue, something gleaned
from the racks of Goodwill.
As I watch, he places a crust in his own mouth,
a communion of wings,
his jaw working with the deliberateness of age.

Before he recedes into the alley,
chickadees, English sparrows,
and the skull-capped bird
whose name I forget,
flit in for this gratuitous offering,
a gift from the gods of snow
that completes the altar of this moment.

IN DEFENSE OF LETTERS
for Gray Zeitz

From his farm near Braintree, John Adams
wrote that unless he kept a journal
the events of his life passed like flights
of birds across his vision, leaving no trace.

Filling my water tank at the pump stations
this cold November morning, I scan the bluffs
of the Kentucky, trees along the steep slopes
reduced to featherless quills, to walls

of anonymous mulch the color of dried tobacco.
Thirty-four pigeons I count huddled along
the twin power lines that droop and join
at the river's edge. They remind me of fonts

of type lifted from the printer's tray,
their inked spines pressed into the page's
chaste snow, John Adams's migrant
and elusive birds nestling on the wires.

IMAGINING MY OWN DEATH

I can envision many deaths—
stumbling into the cistern
on a July evening after too much
chilled Zinfandel, crickets clicking
their symphonies in the grass.
This is only one of them.

Or, instead of Pliny the Elder
sniffing a fatal whiff
of smoking casserole under Vesuvius,
standing in my own backyard
under the white throat
of a colossal sycamore that snaps
while I ponder the genealogy
of snow or a word to describe
the sounds of falling water.

Or maybe improvising illumination
with a lucifer match
as I crouch in darkness
searching for the petite geyser
escaping from a gas pipe.

But the worst is sitting
in a meeting of the Subcommittee
for Administrative Review
convened to measure the efficiency

of systems and processes,
the sands of the hourglass
sifting into a Mojave
of lost time, irrecoverable moments,
the turning of thousands
of tiny wheels that produce
motion but no movement.

THE ORIGINS OF DUST

Rumi says we are, all of us, rugs
on lines, God beating the dust from us.
That pain mainly teaches us
and makes us wise.
The object is not to humble the rug
but to free it of dust
that settles on flat surfaces,
the sills of windows, neglected desks,
the soul that is unnourished.

Its origins are the great republics
of sand and insects, a mix of pollens,
the scales and fur of wild animals,
our own tired skins—
all reunited with the infinite,
flaking, broken into bits, endlessly renewed.

The Feast of Silence (2017)

THE FEAST OF SILENCE

Rounding a bend of Elkhorn,
I see the first angler,
solitary, standing motionless,
waist-deep in green water,
shafts of saffron light falling short
of the shade in which
he swishes his fly across the stillness,
air about him laden with an aqua muzziness
in which dust motes seem suspended.

Around the next,
I see more of their number,
a pair in a fishing kayak
drawn off in a cove,
another in a floppy hat
hunkered at the water's edge
on a sloping stone
that must have fallen
from the cliffs above
before the first keel scraped Plymouth Rock.

Lost in fisher reveries—
the brief reprieve from jobs,
the raucous levies of family—
they do not seem too anxious for the catch
so much as to feed a patient hunger.

Content to place their lives on hold,
they pause like the dragonfly
lighting on the knuckle
of one paddle hand
to take in the drooping limbs,
the *scree* of the hawk,
the white knot of roots on the sycamore
whose falling leaves are riddled to gauze

by insects—
these things that can never be summed
but only relished as a meal more substantial
than fish, a stay beyond this creek
against the hard symmetries of the world,
beyond the incessant drone of traffic
and the scrapings of famished souls,
as they feel themselves replenished,
feeding on this feast of silence.

MT. VERNON ROAD

As we wind through a tunnel
of leaves on a one-lane road
along which deer outnumber humans,
my friend asks,
"Are people happy living way out here?"

Well, yes and no.

Some would say we're too far from Walmart,
others that we're not far enough.

A TREMBLING IN THE LEAF

It can happen when we glance
into a cove of woods
where there is no discernible breeze.

We see a pocket of leaves stirring,
twirling crazily on their stems,
limbs and other leaves
about them motionless as stone.

This thing for which we have no explanation
we store in our cache of imponderables:

the harshness of fortune,
the indifference of nature,
wind where there is no wind,
this trembling in the leaf.

MEETING AN OLD FRIEND
AFTER 50 YEARS

Like water held in the hose in summer
released as the tap turns
at day's end, a stream jetting forth
in white freshets,
unexpectedly, still warm.

REVELATION

In sawing a plaster teardrop
from the floral ceiling medallion
that withstood gravity for 155 years,
I uncovered, fresh as the day it was drawn,
a pencil line of the long-dead plasterer,
a base mark for an intricate pattern,
scored by a hand that will at midday—
weary, hopeful—unwrap his sandwich
with dusty fingers and find himself some shade.

INSTRUCTION

Appraising what someone learns
from someone's teaching
is like mastering the art
of painting wind,
which we can know only
by the bent or broken limb—
or the motions of things it touches.

WILDNESS

> O! The Joy!
>
> —Journal entry of William Clark on viewing the Pacific

Driving along the ridgetop road,
I glimpse, in a cornfield
of broken stalks and shreds of snow,
two deer, a doe and a buck,
hardly lifting their heads from the stubble
on which they are foraging, their sleek,
bark-colored coats of winter
merging with a backdrop of trees
as their muzzles follow my passing car
until it passes, then dropping their wary gazes
and bending their necks again, at home
in the world as it is despite its jarring metal,
its uncompromising engines, its men
who pretend they are foliage of summer trees.
I feel a tingling that begins in the wrists
and spreads with the joy of them.

New Poems

MASTERING THE LANDSCAPE

"Nature has no outline. Imagination does."

—William Blake

The field knows no end
but boundaries of the eye.
The hazy azure beyond
we must imagine.
Like landscape painters,
we think in frames
while the field spills heedlessly.
Art begins in the fence line
where field meets frame,
where infinity finally kisses form.

DEGAS'S SKETCH OF A RECLINING FIGURE

The head turned sidewise,
her gaze directed elsewhere,
a cove in the smooth terrain
of the brow,
just a suggestion of one eye.

His pencil bends her spine
like the flexed wand of a sapling,
like the curve of a harp,
fingering along the outskirts of form—
the descent from thigh to lower limbs
more an outline of muscle than legs
someone would walk or dance on.

Degas knew that visual potency
lies not in the obvious
nor a vibrant foreground,
and that things seem more, presenting less
as we might imagine a pistol,
aimed not at what we can see
but targets beyond our seeing,
beyond the sketch over which
his fingers hover, still clenching
a stem of obedient graphite,
the model already dressing.

DEGAS

It is not the finished canvas
that holds the eye so much
as the preliminaries—
the tentative or nervous hash marks
of a charcoal sketch or exploratory study,
something unfiltered, just started:
the musculature of a filly's foreleg
without a torso, the toeless foot
of a ballerina's flawless calf,
evidence of the mind and hand
in motion,
the moments preceding commitment
as when the cat stalks
its elusive and velvety prey,
its paw teasing before the pounce.

THE TASK OF RESTORING DEMOCRACY

Rooting through a box of old clothes,
deprived of light and breath for years
and sized to fit a previous self,
I found an old white handkerchief—
threadbare, stained, pitted by moths,
though the fading linen is still creased
in a symmetry that honors the iron.
It's a handkerchief, not a flag,
but the cloth remembers its folds.

ATTENTION

As my photographer friend was leaving
the other day, he stopped, his eye spotting
leaves—maybe a dozen maple leaves—
snared between earth and heaven
in an invisible web whose filaments
spanned a panel of the screened porch
as if gravity was arrested in mid-fall.

For days I passed this curiosity
with as little notice as breathing.
Today those threads and ragged yellow swatches
held us both, released us from the rush
of going at things, of swiping rouge
across the world's blurred face. Fetching
his camera from the car, he snapped
several shots to honor the moment
and preserve this mystery of suspension.

Each click became a souvenir to prod us
toward awakening, nudging us to focus
and halt, at least temporarily, these frenzies
of motion and habitual blindness
by which we navigate the world.
Poems, in their leafing, begin this way.

NIGHT DRIVING

My twin headlights pinch the darkness
with puny beams, switching from bright
to dim as other pencils of light approach
and blind us. Knuckles slack on the wheel,
we trust to faceless metal as we hurtle
through the dark, relieved as each hollow
cartridge whooshes safely past. We feel
that comforting little chuff of displaced air.
Opening our windows, it passes over the skin
like a feathery surf.

Our beams only skim the surface of night's
great pool, never far enough, soon enough,
to spare the possum that thumps below us,
the buck's castanet of clattering hooves.
Their allegiance to field and forest
predates us. Slow to change,
they live as though we are not here.
Tired, lulled by motion, we blunder on,
threading one long stitch of yellow stripe
as we penetrate the darkness.

In trusting this cushion of shadows,
we push the boundaries of faith.
Love, it comes to me,
steers behind such a wheel.

ACCOMMODATION

The wasp that lives in my mailbox
offers a truce.
She won't sting.
I won't swat her comb
of papery tubes.
Once a day we meet in no man's land.
So far,
our messages require no postmarks.

CHRISTMAS MORNING

The unfamiliar window looks out on woods—
dingy, furred, broken by little spits of light.
The first motion I make out
is an enormous buck, his rack
floating in a corona of limbs.
He moves with serenity and assurance,
with the subtlety of water soaking into cloth.
He knows without contrivance or thought
that this place belongs to him,
he to it. No tracks appear
in the dusty skim of snow.
He probes the frigid air in revery
as if shaping winter into words.
He's composing a poem, I tell myself.
No, I correct.
He is the poem.

ACKNOWLEDGMENTS

Most of the poems here are drawn from previous publications, a few, I hope, from books to come. They start with *Bluegrass*, Larkspur Press's first book and mine in 1975. Poems from five additional Larkspur books are printed here: *The Country of Morning Calm, Stone Eye, Rail Splitter, Rare Bird*, and *The Feast of Silence*. Set by hand and beautifully designed by Gray Zeitz, they were published in limited editions, given the sheer amount of labor and attention each requires. Several also appeared in Larkspur's broadside series, a practice that began in England in the eighteenth century and migrated to Benjamin Franklin's America. Jonathan Greene graciously published *Earthbones* and the second edition of *Girty*, a hybrid of historical narrative and poems that I call a novel. *Girty* itself was first published in book form by the Turtle Island Foundation of Berkeley, California, (1977), following two installments in *Adena, A Journal of the History and Culture of the Ohio Valley*, a publication of Kentuckiana Metroversity (1976), edited by Leon Driskell. Other reincarnations of *Girty* appeared in later editions by Gnomon Books (1990), Wind Publications (2006), and most recently, by the University Press of Kentucky (2020). Larry Moore's Broadstone Books graciously published *Rain Shadow* (2014), and Katerina Stoykova's Accents Publishing published some of the poems included here in a chapbook titled *Fading into Bolivia* (1990) I am grateful to Jeff Worley and Mike Moran for their careful, sound advice, and more corrections than I care to admit. I am grateful to them as well as all those cited for publishing my work.

ABOUT THE AUTHOR

Richard Taylor is the author of numerous collections of poetry, two historical novels, and several books relating to Kentucky history, including *Elkhorn: Evolution of a Kentucky Landmark*. A former Kentucky poet laureate, he has received two creative writing fellowships from the National Endowment for the Arts as well as an Al Smith Award from the Kentucky Arts Council. Educated at the University of Kentucky (bachelors and Ph.D. in English), he also holds a masters degree (English) from U.L. and a J.D. from the University of Louisville. Practicing law for a few months, he gave up legal practice, a leave-taking he regards as his gift to the Commonwealth of Kentucky. During graduate school he taught in high schools across Kentucky with the Poetry-in-the-Schools Program through the Kentucky Arts Council, editing an anthology of student writing called *Cloud Bumping*. Embarking on a career in education, he taught at Kentucky State University in Frankfort until retiring in 2008. During that time he taught in the Governor's School for the Arts as well as serving as director of the Governor's Scholars Program on two campuses. He also spent a year in Denmark as a scholar-teacher in the Fulbright Program, also teaching a graduate course at Kangwon University in Korea as well as short periods teaching abroad in England and Ireland in a studies-abroad program. He has received publication awards from the Kentucky Historical Society and the Thomas C. Clark Medallion for his Elkhorn book as well as receiving a Distinguished Professor Award at KSU. Recently retired after fourteen years from Transylvania University as Keenan Visiting Writer, he is co-owner of Poor Richard's Books and lives on a small farm outside Frankfort, Kentucky.

www.ingramcontent.com/pod-product-compliance
Lightning Source LLC
Chambersburg PA
CBHW030154100526
44592CB00009B/277